The art of spirituality

LIVIA ZANCA

Contents

Introduction   13

THE ART OF UNDERSTANDING OUR MIND
Our Mind   19
Journal   23

THE ART OF SHADOW WORK
Shadow Work   27
Journal   31

THE ART OF STAYING OPEN
Staying open   35
Journal   39

THE ART OF TAKING RESPONSIBILITY
Taking Responsibility   43
Journal   47

THE ART OF INTENTION
Intention   51
Journal   55

THE ART OF SMUDGING
Smudging   59
Journal   65

THE ART OF SHOWERS AND BATHS
Showers and Baths   69
Journal   75

THE ART OF BREATHING

Our breath 79

Journal 85

THE ART OF MEDITATION

Our Meditation 89

Journal 95

THE ART OF VISUALIZATION

Visualization 99

Journal 105

THE ART OF PROTECTION

Protection 109

Journal 115

THE ART OF JOURNALING

Journaling 119

Journal 125

THE ART OF BELIEF

Belief 129

Journal 133

THE ART OF VISUAL HEALING

Visual Healing 137

Journal 141

THE ART OF HO'OPONOPONO

Ho'oponopono 145

Journal 149

THE ART OF MUSIC & FLUIDITY

Fluidity through Music 153

Journal 159

THE ART OF MIRROR THERAPY

The mirror   163
Journal   167

THE ART OF CUTTING THE CORD

Cutting the Cord   171
Journal   179

THE ART OF FORGIVENESS

Forgiveness   183
Journal   187

THE ART OF COLORS

Colors   191
Journal   197

THE ART OF CHAKRAS

What are chakras?   201
Journal   213

THE ART OF OPENING YOUR CHAKRAS

Opening your Chakras   217
Journal   223

Conclusion   225
The End   227

This book belongs to:

_____

And I promise to take the time to work on myself, to value myself and to respect myself and most of all, to be gentle with myself as I will make mistakes as they are a part of the lessons.

This book was written with the intention of helping us all find
the meaning of unconditional love,
our super power

Introduction

The purpose of this book is to help you become self-aware, to be able to feel everything... and then nothing.

In order to reach peace of mind, we are not to react to the stresses of everyday life. We do not react to anything that may have been trapped inside of us emotionally.

In life, there will always be chaos, and we cannot control it.

What we control is our reactions to what chaos brings up emotionally and how it affects our moods.

How do we do that? Well, it takes work, real work, time, dedication and mostly a lot of patience.

During this journey, we will be digging deep and discover emotions that we didn't even know were there.

We will feel frustrated and mostly alone.

We will learn during this real work to face, accept, let go and forgive.

We will learn to be detectives, psychologists, gurus, and more, all while balancing that with the other roles the responsibilities of our everyday lives as husbands, wives, professionals, mothers, fathers and a lot more...

The work itself is very powerful. We just need to be conscious of it, to be aware, so nothing gets past our observation.

There are things we can add to life that will help us deal with certain situations, challenges and (most importantly) will allow us to let go of lingering feelings that make us depressed or full of anxiety and stress.

So during this journey of self-discovery, we will learn to accept things as they are instead of how we want them to be. We will learn to meditate and to speak to our soul guides and get answers to our questions.

We create the life that we want through the growth of infinite love for ourselves.

We have to challenge ourselves to invest in the most valuable person we'll ever know: OURSELF!!!

We are worth it, you know.

We are a creator, a producer, a writer...

Let us start writing a script for our life...After all, we are a child of light.

The art of Understanding our mind

Our Mind

A re our thoughts driving us crazy?

Yes, they are, actually.

Our mind is powerful and left unchecked. It will keep invasive and repetitive thoughts on heavy rotation.

The mind is a loud speaker that can trigger our emotions to the point of insanity.

We absorb information from the media, from people and from our daily life, and it plays on our minds over and over.

The mind is also an echo chamber for the thoughts we have about ourselves, and these can be quite haunting.

These are the thoughts we want to understand and let go of.

Most of the time, our thoughts are a reflection of how we feel about ourselves.

If we are insecure about our abilities, our looks, our worth, our mind will echo those insecurities, and we will be tortured by them.

Our mind reprimands us for all our faults and mistakes. It constantly repeats that we are not worthy, that we are not perfect.

Our minds trap us in a loop of negativity, and we have to be very aware of this pattern in order to change it.

To change this pattern, we have to change how we feel about ourselves and be very conscious of what comes up in our mind all the time so we can gently work on it and re-frame it.

We are worthy of everything the Divine has to offer and give us.

Artwork

For this exercise, we are going to close our eyes, and we are going to breathe. We may get some images, and we will draw them out right here.

JOURNAL

_____

_____

_____

_____

_____

_____

_____

_____

_____

_____

_____

_____

_____

_____

_____

_____

_____

_____

_____

_____

_____

_____

_____

_____

_____

_____

The art of Shadow Work

Shadow Work

S hadow work is about revealing what is lying in the darkness of our subconscious.

We are only conscious of so much information in our lives.

The healing has to be about what we don't see, what we don't know.

We do not know it because we do not pay attention to it. We feel guilty about something, but we do not work on the reason for the guilt.

We feel ashamed for something, but we do not work on the reason for the shame.

We accept all of it and then live in denial forever because we do not want to touch on the reasons why. It is a very delicate matter to touch on.

Shadow is where the healing is. We need to be very present to pay attention to what is going on in our mind, our body, our actions and then analyze them and find out why, where, and when all of this happened.

Sometimes though, we cannot find out why because it may be coming from a past life. This doesn't mean that you cannot heal it and let it go. It is obviously affecting your present, so the feeling is there hunting and affecting your life.

Also, if we concentrate on lack, guilt, and sadness, our mind will only take the shape of our state of mind.

It is important to change this in order to heal and to change our circumstances.

We need first to address our inner child. We have to pay attention to how that child is feeling.

Are they scared? Sad? Jealous? Angry?

Are they happy? Smiling? Content?

We need to work on releasing the shadows from our inner child in order to help our present self feel lighter.

We need to do a list of what our Inner Child is grateful for and a list of what makes him/her sad and angry.

The Grateful list is to help you see that even in darkness, there are still always things we can be grateful for.

Once we have the list of what makes us sad, we need to journal the scenarios that brought that child to feel this way. Please journal as many details as possible.

Once you have done that, you can also use Ho'oponopono to let it go.

Once you feel that you have done everything possible to release the challenges from your inner child, you can do the same for your older self.

You can also use the mirror to see and journal what it is that you see. It is very important to describe in your journal as much as possible because you need to use the correct words to identify your feelings.

There are many ways of dealing with stuck emotions, and this book gives you a few ways to do that.

Happy Hunting!

Artwork

For this exercise, we are going to close our eyes, and we are going to breathe. We may get some images, and we will draw them out right here.

JOURNAL

_____

_____

_____

_____

_____

_____

_____

_____

_____

_____

_____

_____

_____

_____

_____

_____

_____

_____

_____

_____

_____

_____

_____

_____

_____

The art of Staying Open

Staying open

I am open to receiving the Divine light into my soul

Staying open is very important, as it is needed to be able to find the issue, the pain?

We cannot work on ourselves if we are not open to working on ourselves.

We have to welcome whatever information comes our way.

This information can come during our meditation, during our sleep, through a friend, a stranger, music, or a movie.

During our self-work, we are going to discover many facets of ourselves, and we will have questions that need answering.

We will need to stay open to receive the information, no matter how crazy we think the information is.

Let us remember that even though 20 people will observe the same object, these 20 people will describe it differently. They will be all right in their description, but because each one is seeing it from a different angle, each will have something different to say about it.

This is why it is important to stay open, to listen to what another person has to say about a situation that you are involved in.

It is also very important to stay open to the environment around you, to what is said about a situation, or a person.

Remember that when we hear the same thing more than once about something or someone, it is usually the Universe warning you. Stay open!

When one person shares their opinion about something or someone, it is an opinion, but if all the people around us repeat the same thing, it is now a message.

Artwork

For this exercise, we are going to close our eyes, and we are going to breathe. We may get some images, and we will draw them out right here.

Journal

_____

_____

_____

_____

_____

_____

_____

_____

_____

_____

_____

_____

_____

_____

_____

_____

_____

_____

_____

_____

_____

_____

_____

_____

_____

_____

The art of Taking Responsibility

Taking Responsibility

W hat does that mean?

Well, it means taking responsibility for every scenario that plays in front of us.

These scenarios are not accidents. They are sent by the Divine to remind us that WE need to deal with the issues and not the person(s) in front of us delivering the message.

Every time something happens in front of us, it is about us.

It can be a person who is being unfair in front of us.

It can be an accident or a person cheating on someone else, or a person being spoiled and having a fit.

You are experiencing this, and therefore, it is yours to deal with no matter the scenario.

These are the laws of the Universe, and this is how the Divine communicates with us.

How do I do this?

To start, we are going to take our journal or a piece of paper, and we are going to start writing the experience and the role that person had in it.

We are going to talk about that person or experience and describe all the things that bother you about it.

You are going to write why all these things bother you and when it started and happened.

Once you have described the whole scenario, and the role that person had in it and how it bothered you and also what bothered you, you are going to copy everything you have written and write it again using I instead of her or him.

Example:

I really don't like this person…She is so mean and loud.

She is this way since I met her. She yelled at my friend for nothing and bla bla bla…

Now, I am going to write:

I am so mean and loud. I yell for nothing and at everyone.

Once you have done that, live with it for a while.

Face it and feel it.

Before bed, you can always ask your guides to show you something, or you can ask them to answer questions that you may have about the scenario.

They are always around us to help us, guide us.

Taking responsibility helps us through our path of growth.

An alcoholic will never seek help unless he admits that he is an alcoholic.

Happy Hunting!!!

Artwork

For this exercise, we are going to close our eyes, and we are going to breathe. We may get some images, and we will draw them out right here.

Journal

The art of Intention

Intention

What is intention?

Well, first, everything starts with an intention.

Intention is the awareness of our actions, our words, and the impact they are going to have on someone.

Intention is so much more important than the outcome.

Intention is saying the words and knowing exactly where these words are coming from.

We are here to get to know our souls.

Every exercise we are going to learn, we will be practicing with the intention of healing.

Intention is the awareness of this action, of every action, every thought, every behavior trait, and every word said.

Intention is linked to karma.

Karma is an unresolved thought, word, or action that we throw to the wind and comes back crashing down.

The Divine doesn't bring us karma. The Divine supports us and wants us to ascend, and the only way to do that is to learn to think, do and say everything coming from a place of love.

Being present and awake is very important to pick up the lessons to learn during the challenges thrown at us.

How do we do this?

We have to be present. Intention demands presence; otherwise, we miss the lessons.

When saying something to someone, let us ask ourselves where in the body the words are coming from.

Is it coming from our hearts or our brain? Is it fear-based? Love-based?

Are we saying these words out of love, envy, hatred, resentment, jealousy, etc....???

There are so many scenarios, but we must be aware of them if we need to let go of the emotion attached to them.

Let us be present and choose to say words of love.

Artwork

For this exercise, we are going to close our eyes, and we are going to breathe. We may get some images, and we will draw them out right here.

JOURNAL

The art of Smudging

Smudging

S mudging is cleansing ourselves, our space and others around us by burning herbs such as white sage, cedar, sweet grass and a few other herbs.

Smudging has been practiced throughout history and by many religions: Buddhists use incense, Native Americans use sage, Catholics use Frankincense and they all do the same thing: wash away any negative energies on a person or a space.

We need to cleanse ourselves and our space before starting our healing work as it purifies it and gets rid of any negative energies.

Throughout the day, we pick up negative energies from others and sometimes even from our own emotions. When we start our meditation, we want to take a "spiritual shower" of sorts, and smudging is the tool to help us do that.

As the negative energy leaves our body, we receive the gift of deep relaxation. It is a beautiful feeling.

Smudging is also used as protection against negative energies coming into our space.

When moving into a new space, it is always a good thing to smudge it.

New space, clean energy, new life.

Different types of smudges:

White sage:

It is a ceremonial smudge that can change the mood and energy of the room and person. It is also used for cleansings and meditations.

Juniper:

It is used for purification for rituals and also to invigorate the body and the mind when drained.

Cedar:

This is used to cleanse and bless a new space as it is great for driving away negative energies in order to attract positive energies and influences.

Mugwort:

Traditionally, this herb is used to cleanse one's energy to get rid of negativity. It is also used to stimulate dreams and is used before bedtime.

Palo Santo or Holy wood:

This wood is used for deep healing and to clear negative energies. It is also used to stimulate creativity and have a deeper connection to the Divine.

Lavender:

Is used for protection, for tranquility, for healing. It increases our clairvoyance and promotes happiness. It is also great for psychic protection and cleansings.

Rosemary:

This herb is associated with male energy, the sun, and fire. It is powerful for the aura and for our space as well. It stimulates the memory centers of the brain too.

Black Sage:

Is used to encourage dreams and visions. It helps promote positive energy in our space as well and is used for its aromatherapy scent.

How do we smudge

The first thing we do is smudge ourselves. The purifying vessel (ourselves) needs to be cleansed in order to cleanse so that we may, in turn, cleanse what is around us.

We light one end of the smudge stick and when it is on fire, we blow out the fire and let the smoke billow from the stick.

We wave the stick around us from the top of our head to the bottom of our feet.

We also repeat prayers while smudging to give it a purpose:

"I am a child of light, and I bless myself with the highest and purest intentions."

We then walk around the house and smudge our space, repeating affirmations to cleanse it.

We smudge doors, windows, mirrors, cabinets, hallways, bedrooms, and bathrooms.

The smoke is not dangerous at all and will not be harmful.

Prayers for smudging yourself:

I am a child of light and any energy that is not supported by the Divine light, go away.

With this smoke, I let go of all negative energies around me and all the fears in me that do not serve me and my space.

For my house:

Negative energy, you cannot stay.

This space is mine and filled with light.

I am a child of light and any energy that is not supported by the Divine light has no place here. Go away!

With this smoke, I let go of all negative energies around me and all the fears in me that do not serve me and my space.

There are many prayers for different purposes that I encourage you to check out online.

With time and practice, you can also compose your own prayers, and it is always with the highest and purest intentions.

Happy Smudging!!!

Artwork

For this exercise, we are going to close our eyes, and we are going to breathe. We may get some images, and we will draw them out right here.

JOURNAL

The Art of Showers and Baths

Showers and Baths

~✦~

We pick up everyone's energies during an encounter with people.

We go to work and interact with co-workers. We take public transportation. We help friends with their challenges. We have our own challenges, and the negative effects all of this has on us.

We accumulate and never do shed this surplus of energy until something happens, and we overreact to something that is so unimportant.

Well, you can have a shower or a bath.

Just like smudging, a bath or a shower can help clear the negative energies we carry.

During your cleansing, it is very important to give it intention, and the way to do that is to say at the start of your shower or bath that this is a cleansing ritual.

"I am cleansing all the negative energy that I have collected in the past few days or weeks or months. I am shedding the negative thoughts, intentions, wishes I have for myself or for others."

Just like everything else we do for our spiritual growth, everything becomes a ritual.

A ritual is an intentional ceremony of prayer, of meditation, of cleansing.

We purposely give it a purpose, a command, to be able to direct the action towards a planned outcome.

It is so important to always cleanse as some negative energies can influence your life, your moods, and the outcome of your plans sometimes.

Ritual #1

If you are having a bath, it is important to clean the tub, to smudge the bathroom and light some candles throughout the space and around the tub too.

You are creating a mood that will help the release of negative energies easier.

Once this is done, you can fill the tub with warmer water and add 2 cups of sea salt and 2 cups of backing soda.

Mix the ingredients with the water to help it dissolve and soak in it for at least 30 minutes.

It will leave you tired and weak, but it is in these moments that we realize how much we carry and how stressed we are.

The next day may be moody and if it is, repeat the process until you feel normal again.

If you do not have a tub, you can mix both ingredients with a carrier oil and cover your whole body with this paste and sit in it for 30 minutes before rinsing.

Ritual #2

For the shower:

As you are having a shower in the morning before work, you can direct the cleansing by letting it know that it is cleansing all the stress and negativity out of your body.

It is important to let your body know that it is ok to let go during this morning ritual.

Benefits

- Quiets down your thoughts in your head
- Releases stress from your body
- Helps calm down

Please enjoy!

Artwork

For this exercise, we are going to close our eyes, and we are
going to breathe. We may get some images, and we will draw
them out right here.

JOURNAL

The art of Breathing

Our breath

I breathe in the light, I breathe out the dark

L et's start with that.

Well, we breathe 22,000 times a day, and we are not even conscious that we breathe that many times or at all. It is done automatically, and we take it for granted.

When we are meditating, we have to be conscious of our breathing as it sets the tone for awareness.

We need to pay attention to our breathing, to how fast or slow we breathe.

Breath in
Breath out

Breathing consciously means that we pay attention to the air coming in and going out of our nose and how long we hold it in our lungs before we let it go.

When we pay attention, we begin to clear a space in our minds and can finally focus on something else other than our thoughts, and this creates a deep and quiet peace.

Getting to this state of mind is so important to our well-being. It gives us a break from the noise and the pain that we feel in our bodies.

So how do we do this???

Well, we pay attention to what is going on within instead of outside.

Let's sit comfortably in a safe and loving place and close our eyes.

We are going to take a deep, cleansing breath, and we are going to pay attention to the air entering through the nose and into our body.

Breathe in slowly
Hold it for a few seconds
Breathe out slowly

By paying attention, we are letting go of the control the mind has on us as we are paying attention to our breath instead.

While breathing in, let us visualize light coming into our body, healing, loving, and trusting.

This light goes into every part of our body, regenerating it and loving it.

As our breath comes out of our body, we visualize it taking with it the stress, disease, insecurities, and burdens we carry.

Our minds will never stop thinking, but we can task it to focus on something else, to get busy concentrating on breathing, so it doesn't think of destructive thoughts.

How to:

We sit comfortably in a very safe space, and we close our eyes.

We pay attention to the air coming in and out of our nose and we start slowing down our breathing.

As we are doing this, we start visualizing the light, the healing flowing into all of our body.

As we breathe out, we visualize the stress, the pain, the discomfort come out with our exhaled breath.

We are always in control.

We breathe in self-worth, happiness, abundance, strength, courage, self-love, calm, and healing.

We breathe in anything we want to breathe in that will benefit our body and our mind.

The Universe supports us and is always present for our well-being.

We breathe out self-doubt, stress, what is lacking, and fear. We breathe out all the insecurities within.

The Universe is here to take away all the insecurities we have within and dispose of them.

Breathe them out....Breathe them all out.

Benefits of Conscious Breathing

- Calms the mind and reduces anxiety
- Balances your emotions and manages food cravings
- Lowers your heart rate and blood pressure
- Manages your anger
- Improves your sleep

Artwork

For this exercise, we are going to close our eyes, and we are going to breathe. We may get some images, and we will draw them out right here.

Journal

The art of Meditation

Our Meditation

I stay still and I listen to what my Soul wants to tell me

Meditation is the process of focusing the mind on a task, an object, or just one thought to help it achieve mental clarity.

It is a training tool to help us be aware of the object of our attention as it can be our breath, a thought, a mantra, or specific parts of our body.

Meditation helps us be aware of who we truly are and helps us connect to Divine.

Meditation brings out our creativity, our gifts, and our power.

Meditation grounds us and shows us clearly who we are and what surrounds us.

Meditation helps us see our weaknesses without judgement and shows us how to improve and grow strong.

We are able to do work on ourselves and constantly grow and push our limits without fears.

Why should we start meditating?

We should start meditating to grow emotionally strong, to trust ourselves, to hear the voice of our intuition and to trust it, to help us transform into the truly gifted, loving Souls that we are, and to strengthen our connection to Divine.

We are never alone. Our ancestors, Soul guides are always around to support us, to cheer for us.

Through meditation, we feel the energy within and how to use it. We see what we truly are: the glorious, powerful being that was created through the Divine.

We appreciate and reaffirm that we are enough and that we have everything that we need, and we learn to be grateful for who we are and what we have.

How do I start?

We need a safe, loving spot to meditate.

We can meditate lying down or sitting.

We pay attention to our breath and start slowing it down.

We visualize the stress in our bodies and transform it into something tangible: little balls, little minions, creatures, anything real and dimensional. Once we create a visual representation for our stress, we can visualize that stress leaving our bodies and being absorbed by Mother Earth or the Divine.

As it leaves, we can feel a lightness, a warmth, a peaceful state of mind and body that we should be in all the time.

This inner peace is the goal that we want to reach permanently.

It is very important that we stay open to everything that comes to us during our meditation. There is no place for judgement during this sacred time.

We pay attention to our thoughts and where they lead us.

Old traumas can arise here, but we give it healing light of the Divine and let it go.

We can also repeat healing mantras during our meditation to help us let go and forgive certain emotional pains.

And voila, we are meditating. Easy, right?

The benefits of meditation

Meditation helps with:

- Self-awareness
- Boosts happiness
- Sharpens your focus
- Controls addictions
- Reduces stress
- Improves your mood
- And have a better sleep

Artwork

For this exercise, we are going to close our eyes, and we are going to breathe. We may get some images, and we will draw them out right here.

JOURNAL

The art of Visualization

Visualization

I see the support, the love, the health and the confidence that my soul gives me

Visualization is the formation of a mental image in our mind.

It is the most powerful tool to have in our healing, in our lives.

It can be used for everything.

We can manifest healings, success, abundance and prosperity.

We can visualize breaking down limitations, doubts, hurts and pain.

When we visualize our day-to-day, our life, and our dreams, we are setting the tone for what we want.

Visualization is the language to the Divine.

This is how we ask for what we dream for.

The Divine also communicates through our visualization.

It will show us through a dream, a vision.

It will make us feel it as well, and sometimes it will just bring a stranger with answers.

In order to heal, we have to be able to go into our body and visualize the pain, the limitations, and the doubts to be able to heal them.

We get to work visualizing the energy of the Universe, breaking down these walls that we have built during our traumas to protect ourselves.

How to visualize

Well, if you cannot visualize at all, this is how we can start.

Let's start with a cup, a glass, anything really that you love to use every day.

Put it in front of you and look at it until it is imprinted into my brain. Close your eyes and continue to look at it with your mind's eye.

Keep the vision of the object until it becomes easy to bring up.

Choose another object and do the same again and again until all of these are easy to bring up.

We can also visualize a loved one. We can see them in our minds.

We can also visualize a safe place where we want to run to whenever we are meditating, healing, or just relaxing.

We can repeat these exercises as many times as we want.

Once we are completely comfortable with them, we try our visualization during our meditation.

And remember that there are no rights or wrongs during visualization.

How the visions present themselves is just as important as the visions themselves.

We visualize the air going into our nostrils and filling our lungs.

We visualize the sore spots in our body and notice how the stress shows itself as dimensional objects and we breathe.

We visualize each of these objects rolling off and out of our body and after each one leaves, our body is more relaxed and heavier.

We keep doing this meditation with the combination of the visualization until our body is no longer stressed or in pain and we don't feel our body anymore.

Benefits of visualization

- It improves the ability to see your goals and dreams
- It helps you get better at a task by visualizing it first
- It helps alleviate stress and anxiety
- It helps with pain relief

Artwork

For this exercise, we are going to close our eyes, and we are going to breathe. We may get some images, and we will draw them out right here.

Journal

The art of Protection

Protection

I am a child of light and the Divine walks with me

Spiritual protection is very important while meditating and always when feeling apprehensive or stressed.

It is vital to create a safe and loving space to be able to let go of any fears and to know that we are being looked after energetically while we close our eyes and let go of any stress, anxiety, depression and fears.

The more we protect ourselves, the deeper we go into meditation, where we will reap the benefits of it.

We choose a space in our home where we know we won't be disturbed and where we feel safe.

How do I do that

We go to our sacred space and make ourselves very comfortable meditating.

Once we have reached a state of relaxation, we start visualizing ourselves sitting on the ground and the Earth underneath us with the sun shining and warming us. We enjoy and accept the loving rays of the Sun and we breathe.

We then visualize the center of the Earth and its ball of Red Fire energy, its glorious warmth bubbling and ready to protect us.

We visualize the Red energy making its way up towards us, coming up to the surface.

It reaches us and enters our body through our red chakra at the base of our spine.

It fills our whole body with that loving energy of Mother Earth into our whole body and into our heart.

We breathe it

We feel it

We love it

Once this is done, we bring our inner gaze to the Universe/Divine energy and bring it into our body through the top of our head from the Crown chakra and into our whole body and to our heart.

Again, we breathe it

We feel it

We love it

Both energies are now in our heart and we see with our mind's eye that both are now mixing and turning pink.

There is a pink light in our heart, a bubble of love from the Earth and the Divine combined.

We visualize this bubble growing and growing until it comes out of our body and grows to at least 3 feet away from it all around us.

That energy field is now our Divine protection.

We look at it, we feel it, and we visualize that nothing can penetrate this pink bubble of unconditional love.

We are going to familiarize ourselves with this practice as it is going to be our go to whenever we feel uneasy, nervous, and anxious.

Whenever a person is around us that we are not comfortable with, we say the words:

Ground (to the Earth)
Connect (to the Divine)
Protect (with the pink bubble of unconditional love)

This is our little formula of protection.

Benefits to protecting yourself

It is very important to feel safe in our skin, in our space, in order to feel the protection of the Divine.

This is a great way to feel it.

Artwork

For this exercise, we are going to close our eyes, and we are going to breathe. We may get some images, and we will draw them out right here.

JOURNAL

The art of Journaling

Journaling

*I put on paper what I want the Divine to help me with, to take
away, to cleanse and to liberate*

Journaling is the act of decluttering our monkey brain, you
know, that part of the brain that doesn't know when to be
quiet.

Since we are energy, when we write, we take from the soul to
the page.

Well, we do not want to wait until our container is completely
full before we start emptying it, to heal, to let go.

We want to empty that container on a regular basis and
completely.

The act is so liberating. It feels like we just get naked.

We learn to trust ourselves; we learn about our fears, our strengths, our limitations, and our beliefs.

Through writing, we learn to let go of our beliefs and create new ones.

Who knew?

Journaling is one of my favorite methods of letting go, forgiving, and self-discovery.

It is finding our power through the clutter.

It is loving all the good parts and even the bad ones.

It is mostly learning to be honest with ourselves.

Benefits of journaling

- Quiet the mind
- Focusses us and helps with concentration
- Allows us to BE in the present
- Helps us relax
- Lets the pen dictate the adventure

How do I journal

Well, if we have never before put pen to paper, and we do not know what to say, the best thing is to start by describing the event that is hunting our thoughts, the physical act per say.

We want to be as detailed as possible to make sure that all angles are covered.

We may want to stop there to process what has just happened, or we want to continue.

Continuing, we are going to describe how the situation made you feel. There may be a lot of feelings or not, but if we are able to identify them, we are letting go of them.

Let us not forget that it is not as straightforward as that because there are the primary feelings, and then we have the secondary feelings caused by the primaries and so on.

This is why it takes so long sometimes to heal from that one event.

Once you have written these events, more will come.

Keep journaling!

It will become easier and easier to write your story and to let it go.

If someone is a major key to this story and you arbore any negative feelings toward that person, describe their part in it, how he or she has made you feel, and then surround them in the beautiful pink light of unconditional love and surrender them to the Divine.

This is the best way to deal with this type of situation.

Let them go with love as no karma is created, and we can journal all of this as well.

The lesson in journaling is to learn to communicate with ourselves to get to know who we truly are without shame, guilt, resentment, or dislike.

Let us give ourselves permission to let it all go.

Artwork

For this exercise, we are going to close our eyes, and we are going to breathe. We may get some images, and we will draw them out right here.

JOURNAL

The art of Belief

Belief

I believe that I can change and manifest everything

B elief is a feeling of being sure that a thought is true. It is not based on facts and cannot be validated with physical proof.

These beliefs are usually attached to an experience that was emotionally impactful.

If a person crosses a line and it is a painful experience, we are going to believe that maybe this happened to us because we are not worthy of having love or respect.

These thoughts are not based on any facts. Nowhere is it written that we should not be worthy, or we should be unlucky for the rest of our life, or we should never be happy.

As a matter of fact, the Divine does want us to live this life happily, abundantly and joyfully.

We just need to believe it too.

If there is a belief that is stopping us from progressing or growing, we need to let go of it.

How do I change a belief

Well, we need to choose a limiting belief and write it.

We then write WHY it is a belief.

Where does it come from?

Who played a role in creating that belief?

Once the belief is dissected, we have to ask:

What do I prefer to believe?

"I prefer to believe that I love myself, that I respect myself, that I am worthy, that I manifest the life that I want".

I believe...

When changing the belief in our minds, we are reprograming our brain to believe something else.

Why not make it a positive belief?

It benefits our lives and our well-being.

It also breaks down limitations that we have put on ourselves due to that particular belief.

Benefits of changing a belief

- It helps create movement in my life and brings on shifts.
- I am never stagnant as I constantly learn.
- I get to feel that I am brave and powerful to believe that I can change my life.
- I start to feel strong and worthy of peace and joy.

Artwork

For this exercise, we are going to close our eyes, and we are going to breathe. We may get some images, and we will draw them out right here.

JOURNAL

The art of Visual Healing

Visual Healing

I choose to see, to accept, to forgive, to love and to heal

Visual healing is using the power of our imagination to see with our mind's eye the part of our body affected by disease, stress, or anxiety and help facilitate its healing.

It takes imagination, visualization, and, most importantly, belief that it works.

I learned this method through a Tibetan nun who had a workshop teaching this method that she would use with terminally ill cancer patients and got amazing results, saving them from death with it. She travelled around the world to centers to teach and save them.

How does it work

We go into our safe place for our meditation.

We are going to take a pad and colored crayons and place them beside us.

We are going to make ourselves comfortable and close our eyes for our meditation.

When we are deep into it, we are going to go into our body and scan it to find the area affected if any.

Once found, we are going to look at it and notice the shapes and colors of it as it is very important.

We are going to open our eyes, and we are going to draw what we saw: the shape, the color, the intensity.

We are also going to write what it felt like.

Once we have expressed it, we are going to go back to meditation, go back to that area and go back to seeing it, feeling it for a few moments.

Then we imagine a radiant blue healing light coming from the Divine and filling that whole area with that beautiful, intense, and healing light and flooding it with it, breaking down the mass of stuck energy.

We see that area transform, and we stay with it for as long as we can, basking in the glow of the healing light.

Once done, we open our eyes and go back to our paper and draw again what we saw.

We also express it in writing how it felt and how we feel.

We take that paper and hang it in an area that we are going to see all the time. It becomes an affirmation of our healing, our transformation. We will see it all the time, and that will reinforce the healing.

This is a beautiful process and can help heal what we have set our mind to heal.

We are in control of our life, of our body, of our healings.

We manifest good health.

Benefits

- Taking control of our own well-being
- Taking responsibility for our health, our actions, our life
- Strengthening our power

Artwork

For this exercise, we are going to close our eyes, and we are going to breathe. We may get some images, and we will draw them out right here.

Journal

The art of Ho'oponopono

Ho'oponopono

I am ready to let go of any attachment to the past and to forgive myself for my part in it.

It is important to let go, to forgive ourselves and others for being a part of a scenario that caused pain.

It is important to recognize the source of the pain as nothing will let it go until we face it and accept it and forgive it.

One of my favorites method of forgiveness is Ho'oponopono.

It means "to make things right."

It is a Hawaiian practice for forgiveness.

It is a powerful mantra, and during its practice, I have gone from feeling the pain all over my body to completely letting it go and feel light again.

The belief about this practice is that everything that comes to our line of sight in terms of scenarios, feelings, reactions and pains were experienced before in this life or another.

It is taking responsibility for everything that we face, that we hear, that we see and that we feel.

This is the Divine speaking to us and letting us know that we have work to do.

By choosing to practice Ho'oponopono technique, by repeating the mantra until the challenge is no more, we are able to let it go.

Here is the mantra and its meaning:

I love you – (love) I love my body, my God, my Soul, etc......

I am sorry – (Repentance) I apologize for being a part of the scenario.

Please forgive me – (Forgiveness) I ask forgiveness for the remorse, for participating, for my actions.

Thank you - (gratitude) I thank myself for taking responsibility. I thank the Divine for the support, for the lessons and for the love.

Benefits

- It lightens the load that we carry with us
- It relaxes the body and the mind
- It cuts ties with the people involved in the scenarios
- We forgive and let go

Artwork

For this exercise, we are going to close our eyes, and we are going to breathe. We may get some images, and we will draw them out right here.

JOURNAL

The art of Music & fluidity

Fluidity through Music

Music is the language of my soul. It helps me cleanse and feel my soul's energy.

Music is the language of Spirit. When feeling it from the heart and with true and pure intention, music is a spiritual expression. It has vibrations that dislodge blocks and are combined with movement and the mirror. It becomes a great block clearing tool.

Listening to music that reflects our mood can trigger a release of stuck emotions, stress, and bring out our core energy to fill us with pure love, energy and happiness.

When we need to work on ourselves, we can play a piece of music that is deep, and with high vibrations that we connect to so, we can move our body to it, feel it deeply, open our core energy coming from our Orange Chakra and move that energy where the block is. We can visualize the block exploding and dissipating, replacing it with pure white Divine light.

Music can be meditative, hypnotic and very relaxing.

It can also be full of energy and movement.

When we are able to put ourselves in a trance while moving to a piece of music, we are meditating.

We are able to manifest how we want to feel, what we want to create, and bring out the best in ourselves.

Moving to the music enhances the experience by intensifying the feelings and bringing them to the surface.

Conscious movement helps us feel every part of our body and of the energy inside.

Our core energy, located under the belly button, can be awakened and used to heal us and refuel us as well.

This energy is our main resource and never dies.

To be able to use it to heal and energize us is a beautiful and useful tool.

How do I connect to the music and move through it?

The first thing I do is to recognize how I feel.

I choose a piece of music that mimics my feelings.

While playing the piece of music that initial time, I just listen and meditate.

I meditate on it until my body feels like moving.

Then, I start moving my hands, my arms, my shoulders, and I get up to continue moving my chest, my waist, my hips and legs.

I concentrate on the feeling that I need to deal with and through the movement of our body, we can bring it to the surface.

We can also repeat our Ho'ponopono mantra during that time. Play the mantra over and over until that feeling is completely gone.

Moving to the sound of music is very releasing and with practice, we can move the energy everywhere in our body, and it will eliminate the energy blocks we have.

With my eyes closed, I go within to see exactly where that feeling is stuck and as I am moving, I concentrate all my energies on that spot and send a lot of love to it.

I go through my whole body doing this, and then I sit again and let the love flow through me.

Why should I do this?

Well, music opens the heart and connects to the feeling at hand and with love.

It elevates the mood and reduces stress.

It manages pain and stimulates the memories of the cause of it and brings them to the surface so we can release them.

With the movement, I am able to bring my core energy to the area where the feeling is stuck and drown it with positive light before letting it go.

You can also use your voice to determine the right sound that will reach the block and voice that sound to release it.

You can put your hand in the area to reach so you can better feel the sound within.

Music helps visualize and create as well.

Enjoy!

Artwork

For this exercise, we are going to close our eyes, and we are going to breathe. We may get some images, and we will draw them out right here.

Journal

The art of Mirror Therapy

The mirror

Mirror, Mirror on the wall, who's the truest of them all

The mirror is a great tool for getting to know oneself.

We are able to look at everyone in front of us and what they do, but we hardly have a chance to look at ourselves, truly observe how we behave from a day to day unless we carry a mirror in front of us at all times.

The mirror is brutally honest and smacks us with the truth every time, and this is why this method is amazing for getting to know oneself.

When we are going through something, but we are not exactly sure what it is, it is always good to go in front of the mirror and observe ourselves until the feeling is right in front of us and we can see it, recognize it and let it go.

During our mirror session, certain fear-based emotions will make us look down because of shame, guilt, or denial as well.

We need to look again to get to know these feelings so we can recognize them in others or ourselves.

We will know how it looks and feels.

If we stay long enough, we are able to become comfortable with it, accept it, and let go of it.

It is very important to choose a mirror that is beautiful to us, a mirror that we want to look at, a mirror that attracts us.

How does it work

Well, as I said, when we are not feeling our best, we go to our beautiful mirror, and we put on the music that is in tune with our feelings.

We can dance in front of the mirror first to strengthen the intensity of the feelings and to pay attention to the location of the feeling we are going to deal with.

We continue to dance, and we connect with our core energy and open the floodgates so we can feel the intensity of it.

Once this energy is out, we direct it to the area where the pain is located, and we give it our spirit love.

We can also repeat the Ho'oponopono mantra as well.

During this whole process, we look at ourselves in the mirror, we pay attention to our moves, our feelings, our looks, our pain and our releases.

We can also just sit in front of the mirror and just look at ourselves and observe what is going on, looking straight into our soul through our eyes.

When it feels intense, we can repeat our beautiful mantra until it is no longer intense.

Benefits

- We get to know ourselves
- We learn to recognize different emotions and behaviors
- We forgive ourselves and others for our parts in a lesson
- We learn to trust ourselves

Artwork

For this exercise, we are going to close our eyes, and we are going to breathe. We may get some images, and we will draw them out right here.

JOURNAL

The art of Cutting the cord

Cutting the Cord

I cut the ties between my past and my present, so I can move on

Attachment is normal in humans. We have children, we want to protect them and guide them properly, and we tend to overprotect them as we think that loving them is to project our fears onto them.

Spiritual love, on the other hand, is detached and free.

It is ok to let our loved ones make their own decisions.

It is ok for them to decide who they want to be without interference from anyone else around them.

Unfortunately, this doesn't happen often.

We accumulate experiences, and feelings for people that can be negative and harm us.

Cutting the cord is a very important part in the healing process. It is important to let go of the past, of the people who have hurt us, and of situations that were traumatic.

When our pain, our past, does not cloud us, we are able to concentrate on the NOW.

We are able to enjoy what is going on in our lives right at this moment.

Memories of happiness are, after all, what we live for.

Remember that forgiveness is not for others, it is for ourselves.

Let us start cutting the cords with everyone or everything that reflects pain.

How do we do that

Well, the best thing to do is to draw a stickman representing you and one representing the other person, if it is a person.

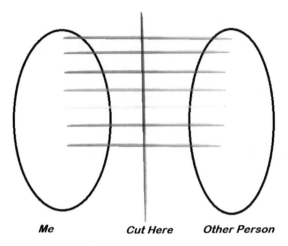

Me   **Cut Here**   **Other Person**

Write everything that connects you to that person

We surround each one with the Divine light and add the chakras in their rightful place.

Connect each of your chakra to the ones of the other person with a line.

Write what connects you to that person under the drawings.

Take a pair of scissors and cut between the chakra lines, and you can say out loud:

I cut the cords between you and me.
With love I release what connects you to me.
I thank you for the lessons, and I set you free.
The ties that connected us are now cut, and we are each free to go our own separate ways.

Now when performing the cutting of the cord with an event, you, of course, do not draw a stick man for the second drawing but just a bubble of light with the event name under it, and you still connect each chakra together.

You will also describe the even beside the drawing to make sure that the cutting is exactly for that event.

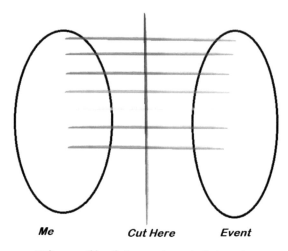

Me   **Cut Here**   **Event**

Write everything that connects you to that event

Happy Cutting!

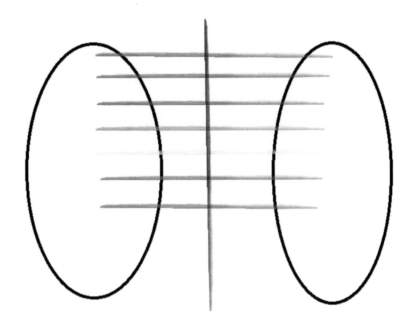

Artwork

For this exercise, we are going to close our eyes, and we are going to breathe. We may get some images, and we will draw them out right here.

Journal

The art of Forgiveness

Forgiveness

"As per psychologists, forgiveness is a conscious, deliberate decision to release feelings of resentment or vengeance toward a person or group who has hurt you or harmed you, regardless of whether they actually deserve your forgiveness or not."

Forgiveness is deeper than that. It is about ourselves and learning to be gentle with ourselves and forgiving ourselves for participating in a scenario that ended up hurting us.

The hurt usually is attached to a lesson.

What is the lesson, you say?

Well, this is where your inner inspector Clouseau comes in.

Who hurt you? How did they hurt you? What triggered that hurt?

Obviously, if there was a reaction from you, it is because there were some past hurts that relate to the present scenario.

Usually, if we do not have a reaction, there are no issues.

The moment that our body, our emotions react to something that is presented in front of us, then there is an attachment to a past issue, pain that is stuck within.

The important thing is to find it, understand it and forgive it.

But how?

Meditate on it.

Bring forward the person or the event that played a part in it that consumes your energy.

Visualize this person being in front of you. Have a clear picture of him or her.

Then I want you to imagine that person being two years old.

Visualize the person shining with the white light of the Divine, being a part of the divine, having been chosen to hurt you in order to teach you a lesson.

It is quite the responsibility to choose to be a part of someone else's lesson.

Surround him or her with light. Understand that they are part of your journey and your lesson.

Journal everything surrounding the event and the people who played a role in it, and the role you played in it as well. Do not forget to take responsibility for your own actions and be very honest with all of it.

Cut the cords. Ho'oponopono the feelings that come up to the surface for yourself and for the others.

Let it go so it doesn't hurt you in the future.

Benefits of Forgiveness

- Being gentle with your soul
- Freedom
- Kindness to yourself as you do not have to suffer the pain caused by the event or the person
- Taking responsibility for your part in the event
- Liberating all the stuck feelings

Artwork

For this exercise, we are going to close our eyes, and we are going to breathe. We may get some images, and we will draw them out right here.

JOURNAL

The art of Colors

Colors

I am turning everything into the colors that resonate with my soul

We are surrounded by colors all day long, and we don't even pay attention to them anymore.

We are so busy with our lives that we do not take the time to enjoy our surroundings.

We talk about the colors that we love and the ones that we don't like at all, but we do not understand why we do not like them.

All these colors are energy, and we have them in our field of energy.

If we do not like one of them, it could be because it is attached to a memory or a block.

This particular color is attached to a painful experience or a blockage in one of our chakras.

How do we know?

Well, sometimes, we do not know where it is coming from, but from my experience, I have found that if we surround ourselves with a color that we do not like, it only takes about a week or two at the most to get over it.

Do we have the courage to face what comes up?

I have spent most of the last five years facing memories or blocks by surrounding myself with a particular color.

I would paint my room every 3 to 6 months, depending on how fast the healing happened.

I do have to say that when I was younger, I didn't like green and purple at all.

Having applied them in my home, I am good with these colors now as I have healed the feelings that were attached to them.

The great thing with colors is that you still get a healing, but it is subliminal healing as you do not even pay attention to what is going on as the color is there, surrounding you, nourishing you and healing you.

I am not telling you to paint your room every 3 to 6 months, but you can use a board with a particular color, look at it, feel it and meditate on it.

Here are the psychological meanings of each color:

Purple: (Crown chakra)
Positive: vision, high consciousness, intuition, spiritual awareness, royalty, inner peace, ancient wisdom, forgiveness
Negative: emotional, arrogant, immature, overly vigilant

Indigo: (third eye chakra)
Positive: vmotions, subconscious, Intuition, insight, sensitivity, deep-inner knowing
Negative: fragile, timid, arrogant

Blue: (throat chakra)
Positive: loyalty, honesty, dependability, confidence, trust
Negative: controlling, pompous, tense

Green: (heart chakra)
Positive: harmony, growth, Prosperity, hope, balance
Negative: judgmental, envious, materialistic

Yellow: (Solar Plexus chakra)
Positive: happiness, creativity, inspiration, optimism
Negative: cowardice, egotistic, deceptive

Orange: (Sacral Chakra)
Positive: optimism, warmth, spontaneity, creative
Negative: exhibitionist, superficial, impatient, domineering

Red: (Root chakra)
Positive: sexual, full of life, confident, passionate
Negative: aggressive, impulsive, domineering

Pink:
Positive: unconditional love, romance, innocence, feminine
Negative: childish, unrealistic, not confident

Taupe:
Positive: neutral, influences, triggers, comforting
Negative: close-minded, dull, abstinent, doubtful

Brown:
Positive: natural, stabilizes, common sense
Negative: suppresses emotions, dull, unsophisticated

Grey:
Positive: lunar magic, clairvoyance, practical, protection
Negative: tired, mental weakness, conformism

Gold:
Positive: healing energy, self-confidence, self-worth, elegance, attracts, motivates, generous, healing
Negative: selfishness, arrogance, controlling, materialistic, egotistic

Silver:
Positive: purity, values, female energy, affluence
Negative: deceiving, immoral, insincere

White:
Positive: peace, cleansing, higher self, spirituality, decluttering, innocence
Negativity: cold, sterility, plain, isolation, emptiness

Black:
Positive: Power, authority, control, discipline
Negative: controlling, creates fear, intimidates

Artwork

For this exercise, we are going to close our eyes, and we are going to breathe. We may get some images, and we will draw them out right here.

JOURNAL

_____

_____

_____

_____

_____

_____

_____

_____

_____

_____

_____

_____

_____

_____

_____

_____

_____

_____

_____

_____

_____

_____

_____

_____

_____

The art of Chakras

What are chakras?

◗◖∽◗◖

Chakras are energy centers. There are 7 of them, and they are located along the spine. They start at the root all the way to the top of the head.

These spinning energy wheels each correspond to a certain part of the body, nerves, and organs.

In order to function at their best, it is important that they are balanced.

If they are not, the person may experience emotional, spiritual, and physical discomfort.

Root chakra: Red

Mantra: I am

Element: Earth

Frequency: 396 Hz

Crystals: Hermetite, smoky quartz, bloodstone, red jasper, black tourmaline

Oils: Patchouli, Juniper, Sandalwood, Myrrh, Vetiver, Frankincense

It is located at the base of the spine, and it provides a foundation for life. It is through it that you ground yourself to the Earth and are able to deal with challenges.

It is responsible as well for your security and stability.

What blocks the Root chakra: Trauma, poor bonding with parents, abuse, neglect

Blocked: fearful, anxious, unsure, financial instability, ungrounded

Balanced: Safe, secure, centered, grounded, happy to be alive

Overactive: greedy, lust for power, aggressive, materialistic, cynical

To unlock it: stretch, yoga (root poses), take a shower, meditate, envision the color red, walk outdoors barefoot, chant the sound UUUUUHHHHHHH

Affirmations:

I deserve success

I am worthy of love, of dreaming and of abundance

I am supported

I am loved

I am grounded

SACRAL CHAKRA: ORANGE

Mantra: I feel

Element: Water

Frequency: 417 Hz

Crystals: Carnelian, Orange Calcite, Sunstone, Amber, Citrine

Oils: Jasmine, Rose, Ylang Ylang, Sandalwood, Cardamom, Orange Clary Sage

It is located just below your belly button. It is responsible for your sexual and creative energy.

It is also responsible for how you relate to your emotions and to others' emotions.

What blocks the Sacral: Ignored feelings, severe religious programming, abuse, manipulation

Blocked: low libido, fear of intimacy, no creativity, isolated

Balanced: Passion, Creative, healthy, libido, optimistic, open

Overactive: Over emotional, fixated on sex, hedonistic, manipulative

To unlock your Sacral Chakra: Citrine, Yoga (sacral poses), eat oranges, meditate, positive affirmations, drink more water, chant the sound OOOOOOOO

Affirmations:

I am worthy

I am a work of art

I allow my inner self to be seen and expressed

SOLAR PLEXUS CHAKRA: YELLOW

Mantra: I do

Element: Fire

Frequency: 364 Hz

Crystals: Citrine, Tiger's Eye, Lemon Quartz, Sunstone, Yellow Jasper, Aragonite

Oils: Aniseed, Ginger, Lemon, Rosemary, peppermint, pine

The Solar Plexus is located in your stomach and is responsible for confidence and self-esteem.

It also helps you feel like you are in control of your life. It also allows you to set and keep boundaries.

Deepest connections with willpower, self-discipline.

Blocked: Low self-esteem, feeling powerless, inferiority complex

Balanced: Confident, feel in control, personal power, drive, good self-image

Overactive: Power hungry, domineering, perfectionist, critical

To unlock your Solar: Amber crystals, Yoga (solar plexus poses), meditate, chamomile tea, positive affirmations, chant the sound OOOHHHHHHHH

Affirmations:

I am proud of me

I accept myself unconditionally

I am confident in all aspects of my life

I respect and honor my needs and boundaries

Heart Chakra: Green/Pink

Mantra: I love

Element: Air

Frequency: 128 Hz

Crystals: Rose Quartz, Jade, Rhodonite, Green Calcite, Pink Moonstone

Oils: Bergamot, lavender, cinnamon, rose, Jasmine

It serves as the center of love for oneself and others, compassion, empathy and forgiveness.

It is associated with unconditional love, joy and compassion. It is the source of deep and profound truths that cannot be expressed with words.

Blocked: Lack of empathy, bitter, hateful, trust issues, intolerant

Balanced: Peaceful, loving, compassionate, tolerant, warm, open

Overactive: Jealous, codependent, self-sacrificing, giving too much

To unlock your heart: Rose Quartz, yoga (heart poses), meditate, green foods, wear green clothes, affirmations, chant the sound AAAAHHHHHHH

. . .

Affirmations:

It is safe for me to trust myself and others

I deserve love

I accept myself

I live my life in alignment with my heart

THROAT CHAKRA: BLUE

Mantra: I speak

Element: Ether

Frequency: 192 Hz

Crystals: Blue Calcite, Blue lace Agate, Aquamarine

Oils: Birch, lavender, Oregano, sage, tea tree, Eucalyptus, chamomile

The throat chakra is located at the base of the neck and is the center of communication, creativity and emotions. If unbalanced, you may not be able to be honest or to express your thoughts. It expresses your will as well as your mental and emotional intentions.

Blocked: Cannot express yourself or speak out, misunderstood, secretive, and doesn't listen well.

Balanced: Confident, expressive, clear communicator, creative, diplomatic

Overactive: opinionated, loud, critical, gossipy, yell or talk over others, harsh words

To unlock your throat chakra: Lapus Lazuli, yoga (neck poses), meditate, blueberries, affirmations, chant the sound EEEEYYYYYYEEEE

Affirmations:

I express myself freely

I speak my truth with love

I listen as well as I express myself

I honor my voice, my ability to express myself

THIRD EYE CHAKRA: INDIGO

Mantra: I see

Element: Light

Frequency: 144 Hz

Crystals: Sodalite, Labradorite, Lapis Lazuli

Oils: Clary sage, cypress, sandalwood, vetiver, frankincense

The third eye chakra is located in the center of your head, parallel to the middle of your eyebrows. It represents perception, awareness, and spiritual communication. When it is open, you are gifted with clairvoyance, visions, and extrasensory perceptions.

Blocked: Poor judgement, lack of focus, poor imagination, cannot see beyond the physical.

Balanced: Imaginative, intuitive, clear thoughts and vision, sees beyond the physical.

Overactive: Nightmares, delusions, hallucinations, obsessive, seeing too many spirits

How to unlock your third eye: Amethyst, yoga (headstands and inversions), meditating, dark chocolate, look at the stars, chant the sound AAAAYYYYYYYYY

Affirmations:

I trust myself and my intuition

I am open to the wisdom within

I nurture my spirit

I am connected to the Divine

CROWN CHAKRA: PURPLE

Mantra: I know

Element: Cosmos

Frequency: 216 Hz

Crystals: Amethyst, Selenite, Clear Quartz, Moon stone, Spirit Quartz

Oils: ginger, basil, Neroli, jasmine, Ylang Ylang

The Crown Chakra is located at the top of your head and is the connection between Spiritual and physical.

It lifts and inspires you. It connects you to the Divine and makes you realize your own divinity and that you are a soul in a physical body.

Blocked: Depression, learning difficulties, weak faith, anger at the Divine, brain fog

Balanced: Strong faith, universal love, intelligence, awareness, wise, understanding

Overactive: Dogmatic, judgemental, addictions, ungrounded

How to unlock the Crown Chakra: Clear Quartz, yoga (inversions), mantras affirmations, meditate, ginger, herbal teas, chant the sound EEEEEEEE

. . .

Affirmations:

I am a divine being

I am infinite

I am divinely guided and inspired

I come from a place of love and understanding

JOURNAL

The art of Opening your chakras

Opening your Chakras

When we suspect that one or all chakras are not working the way they should, we need to address the problem.

Slow-moving or completely blocked chakras can cause many physical or emotional problems such as loneliness, anger, low self-esteem and having difficulties making decisions and many more.

To deal with that, we are going to do a meditation for our chakras to kick start them.

We sit in our comfortable meditation space, and we start our breathing and relaxation.

Once we are in deep meditation, we are going to do our protection meditation.

We are then going to visualize at the top of our head the Crown Chakra, purple sparkler lit and going in circles.

It shines, it sparkles, and it is alive. This is your connection to the Divine and you can feel the energy connecting you to it.

You feel the energy in that spot, and you hold on to it.

Once you are comfortable with the energy in that spot, you are going to go to the Third Eye Chakra, and you are going to visualize an Indigo sparkler going in circles as well and shining gloriously and filling the penial gland with energy.

Feel the connection to the area of the eyes, nose, and pituitary gland. This area is about truth, power of the mind and control.

Before going to the next chakra, you are going to visualize the purple sparkler, and then the Indigo sparkler, and then you are going to bring your attention to the Blue chakra sparkler turning in circles and filling your throat with energy. Feel the energy and love it.

Connect to the blue energy as it is about speaking your truth. It is about repressed words, opinions and emotions. Visualize them flowing out of your throat.

Again before going to the Heart chakra, you need to go back to the purple, then the Indigo, and then the Blue chakras before concentrating on the green heart chakra sparkler.

It shines and makes circles with it. You can feel the green energy filling your heart with love, with sparkles, with energy.

This connection is about the power of love and emotions, the ability to nourish yourself, and to receive or give love and intimacy.

After having completed the Heart Chakra, you go back to the beginning and start again from the top of the head and go through all the chakras that are sparkling, and you stop at the Solar Plexus Chakra and visualize the Yellow Sparkler going in circles and shining with brilliance. Feel that energy and give it love.

Connecting to the yellow chakra brings you power, self-esteem and trust. Feel these and fill yourself with their energy.

You then go back to the beginning, going through each chakra before getting to the Sacra Chakra.

It is shining with a brilliant orange sparkler, feeling the power of your energy flowing through it.

This connection is about the power of relationships, sexuality and creativity.

Go back to the top of the head and just observe the open chakras sparkling one by one until you get to the Red chakra.

When you get to your Red chakra, visualize it sparkling red and in circles. Feel the energy at the bottom of the spine getting more and more intense.

Feel the connection to that chakra as it brings grounding, pride, ego, self-image, safety and security.

Once you have done this work of opening all the chakras, you can wait a while to feel the energy to get used to it and the higher vibrations.

Once you are done, you can go back to the red chakra and extinguish the red sparkler, then the orange one, the yellow one, and so on until they are all turned off.

I would do this exercise at least once a day, every day, to help your chakras function normally.

It is important, though, to close them after the exercise because when you open them, you are opening them to the Divine for healing and guidance.

If you do not close them after your meditation, you are exposing yourself to all kinds of energies that may not be so pleasant and may be harmful energetically.

Another way to look at the chakras is as a flower opening and then closing.

Artwork

For this exercise, we are going to close our eyes, and we are going to breathe. We may get some images, and we will draw them out right here.

Journal

Conclusion

I hope you enjoy these exercises as much as I still do.

They show us that we are a powerful being, what we are capable of, and that we are in control of ourselves, of our own healings and of our happiness.

They show us that we are all children of the light and that when we come from a place of purity and goodness, we can manifest everything we want.

Our imagination is a great tool to achieve our dreams, our goals, and the life we want to live.

I leave you with love, and I encourage you to continue to work on building your power and be the extraordinary being that you deserve to be.

With love.

The End

Manufactured by Amazon.ca
Bolton, ON

26994219R00127